New Canaan Library

151 Main Street
New Canaan, CT 06840

(203) 594-5000
www.newcanaanlibrary.org

OCT 23 2006

Beginning to END

Flower To Honey

A Buddy Book

by

Julie Murray

ABDO
Publishing Company

VISIT US AT
www.abdopublishing.com

Published by ABDO Publishing Company, 4940 Viking Drive, Edina, Minnesota 55435.

Copyright © 2007 by Abdo Consulting Group, Inc. International copyrights reserved in all countries. No part of this book may be reproduced in any form without written permission from the publisher. Buddy Books™ is a trademark and logo of ABDO Publishing Company.

Printed in the United States.

Coordinating Series Editor: Sarah Tieck
Contributing Editor: Michael P. Goecke
Graphic Design: Maria Hosley
Cover Photograph: Media Bakery, Photos.com
Interior Photographs/Illustrations: Art Explosion, Clipart.com, Getty Images, Media Bakery, Photos.com

Library of Congress Cataloging-in-Publication Data

Murray, Julie, 1969–
    Flower to honey / Julie Murray.
        p. cm. — (Beginning to end)
    Includes index.
    ISBN-13: 978-1-59679-836-6
    ISBN-10: 1-59679-836-X
    1. Honey—Juvenile literature. 2. Cookery (Honey)—Juvenile literature. I. Title.

TX560.H7M865 2006
641.6'8—dc22

                                                                    2006019895

Table Of Contents

Where Does Honey Come From? 4

A Starting Point 8

Time For Gathering 11

Fun Facts 14

Creating Honey 16

From Hive To Table 18

Can You Guess? 22

Important Words 23

Web Sites 23

Index 24

Where Does Honey Come From?

Honey is an important product. Many people like to eat honey. It can also be used for baking. Some people even use it to soften their skin. Do you know how honey is made?

Honey is a **natural** product. It is made by bees who gather **nectar** from flowers. The bees take the nectar to their hives. There, they turn it into honey. The honey provides the bees with the food they need to live.

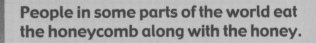

People in some parts of the world eat
the honeycomb along with the honey.

Look at a bottle of honey. You can see what kind of flower the honey was made from. Different flowers make different kinds of honey. **Nectar** from orange blossoms makes orange blossom honey. Nectar from clover flowers makes clover honey.

Honey can be different colors. The color
depends on the flowers used to make it.

A Starting Point

Bees are a type of insect. There are more than 20,000 kinds of bees throughout the world. Bees that make honey are called honeybees.

Honeybees live together in hives. In the hive, bees build a honeycomb from wax. Six-sided holes, called cells, make up the honeycomb. Honey is made there.

Bees make honey in some of the honeycomb cells.

9

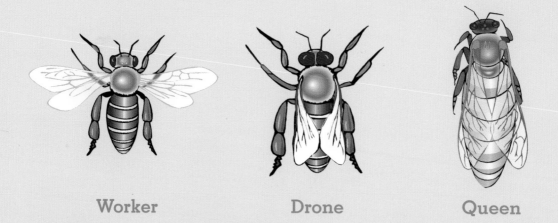

Worker   Drone   Queen

Three different types of bees live within the hive. There are female worker bees, male drone bees, and a female queen bee.

Worker bees gather **nectar** and take care of the hive. Drone bees mate with the queen. The queen bee lays eggs.

Time For
Gathering

Bees have many important jobs in nature. One is to **pollinate** plants. When bees fly from flower to flower, they gather pollen. When pollen is spread around by the bees, new plants grow.

Bees also gather **nectar** from flowers. Nectar is a clear liquid made mostly of water and sugar. Bees use nectar to create their main source of energy, honey.

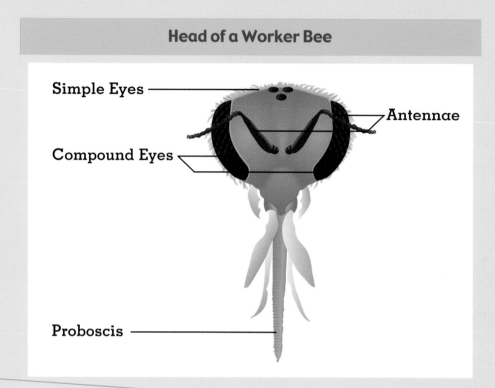

Head of a Worker Bee

Simple Eyes

Antennae

Compound Eyes

Proboscis

Honeybees have a special tongue to help them gather **nectar**. This tongue is like a straw. It is called a proboscis.

A bee uses its proboscis to suck nectar from a flower. Then, the bee takes the nectar back to the hive.

A honeybee's proboscis helps it gather nectar.

FUN Facts
Did you know...

... Most Americans eat about one pound (.45 kg) of honey each year.

... Worker bees live about 30 days. It takes a worker bee its entire life to make 1/12th of a teaspoon of honey.

A bee would see the red in these flowers as green.

... Even though bees have five eyes, they can't see the color red.

... China **manufactures** more honey than any other country in the world.

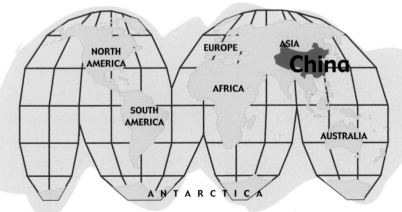

NORTH AMERICA

SOUTH AMERICA

EUROPE

AFRICA

ASIA

China

AUSTRALIA

ANTARCTICA

China is a country on the continent of Asia.

Creating
Honey

Making honey is hard work. It requires the help of all the bees in the hive.

First, worker bees must gather **nectar** from flowers. They store this nectar in their honey stomachs. The honey stomach is a second stomach for storing nectar.

After workers bring the nectar back to the hive, they must share it. They do this by chewing the nectar and dropping it into the honeycomb cells. Then, the workers fan their wings over the cells. This dries out the nectar and changes it into honey.

Body Parts of a Worker Bee

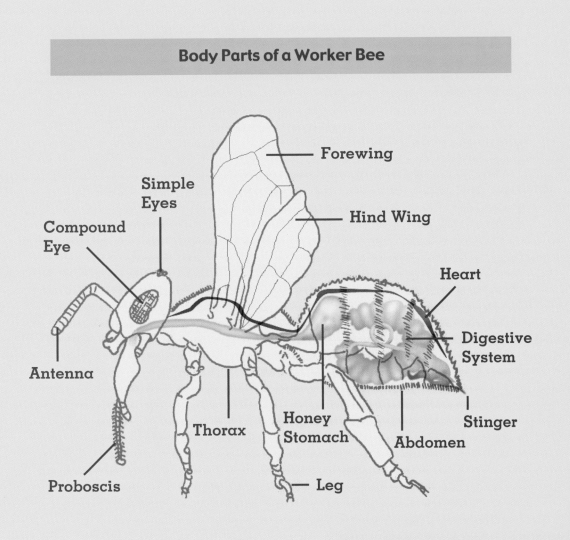

Forewing

Simple Eyes

Compound Eye

Hind Wing

Heart

Digestive System

Antenna

Honey Stomach

Stinger

Thorax

Abdomen

Proboscis

Leg

Bees have many body parts that help them make honey.

17

From Hive To Table

Beekeepers are like farmers. They raise bees for honey. They do this by keeping beehives in special boxes. The boxes can hold many honeycombs at a time. When beekeepers gather the honey from the hives, they wear special clothes. These clothes protect beekeepers from bee stings.

After the honey is collected, a truck picks it up from the beekeeper's farm. Then, the honey is delivered to a **factory**.

Beekeepers wear helmets to cover their faces. They also wear coveralls, boots, and sometimes gloves to protect their skin.

Machines at a **factory** put honey into bottles. Then, the honey can be sold to stores. Stores often sell many kinds of honey. People buy the honey they want and take it home to eat.

Next time you spread honey on a piece of bread, think about its journey from hive to table.

Machines at a factory can bottle many jars of honey at once.

Can You Guess?

Q: What is the queen bee's job in the hive?

A: She lays eggs.

Q: Which U.S. state is sometimes called "The Beehive State"?

A: Utah.

Important Words

factory a business that uses machines to help with work.

manufacture to make.

natural from nature.

nectar a sweet liquid that flowers make, similar to sugar water.

pollinate to bring pollen to many flowers.

Web Sites

To learn more, visit ABDO Publishing Company on the World Wide Web. Web site links about this topic are featured on our Book Links page. These links are routinely monitored and updated to provide the most current information available.

www.abdopublishing.com

Index

Americans 14

antennae 12, 17

Asia 15

baking 4

bee . . .4, 8, 9, 10, 11, 12,
    13, 14, 15, 16, 17, 18, 22

beekeeper 18, 19

bottle 6, 20, 21

bread 20

cells 8, 9, 16

China 15

clothes 18, 19

clover 6

eyes 12, 15, 17

factory 18, 20, 21

flowers 4, 6, 7, 11,
    12, 15, 16

hive 4, 8, 10, 12, 16,
    18, 20, 22

honey stomach . .16, 17

honeycomb 5, 8, 9,
    16, 18

nectar 4, 6, 10, 11,
    12, 13, 16, 18

orange blossom 6

pollen 11

pollinate 11

proboscis 12, 13, 17

skin 4, 19

store 20

Utah 22

wax 8

wings 16, 17